BY HAZEL BAUTISTA QUIAMAS

— simply recipes —

COOKBOOK

All global publishing rights are held by

Ukiyoto Publishing

Published in 2023

Content Copyright © Hazel Bautista Quiamas

ISBN 9789359201054

All rights reserved.
No part of this publication may be reproduced, transmitted, or stored in a retrieval system, in any form by any means, electronic, mechanical, photocopying, recording or otherwise, without the prior permission of the publisher.

The moral rights of the author have been asserted.

This book is sold subject to the condition that it shall not by way of trade or otherwise, be lent, resold, hired out or otherwise circulated, without the publisher's prior consent, in any form of binding or cover other than that in which it is published.

**GLOBAL TASTE OF KOREA 2017
2ND PLACE FREESTYLE
COOKING**

Contents

Twinkling stars **Error! Bookmark not defined.**

When papa fell in the puddle **Error! Bookmark not defined.**

Summer, stay with me! **Error! Bookmark not defined.**

When mummy scolded me**Error! Bookmark not defined.**

Summer holidays**Error! Bookmark not defined.**

Reach for the stars **Error! Bookmark not defined.**

My favourite pie **Error! Bookmark not defined.**

School bus ride **Error! Bookmark not defined.**

My baby brother **Error! Bookmark not defined.**

About the Author 1

Cooking, sometimes known as the art of cooking, is the art and science of preparing food for human consumption. Cooking techniques and ingredients differ from location to place and from person to person. There are several varieties of gas stoves used for cooking meals, including electric stoves, gas stoves, ovens, and even baked Chulhas.

The origins of cooking are unknown, however our forefathers or early humans invented fire and gradually began utilizing it to prepare their meals. Previously, humans used clay pots as receptacles in which to prepare their food. Previously, people were unaware of so many different sorts of food, and they only utilized fire to prepare raw meat.They obtained by hunting animals. Cooking processes and the cooked meal list have evolved with time and human evolution.

"As I joined the Global Taste of Korea 2019 I decided to make a Kimchi Jiggae with Blue and Red Tofu and Yellow egg yolk that represents the flag of the Philippines blue red and yellow symbolized the friendship of filipino and korean culture."

- Hazel Quiamas

Cooking is a beautiful hobby that many people like. It is the ability and art of enhancing the taste, flavor, and appearance of food. It has been practiced since ancient times and has now become an essential component of our daily life. It is not only about cooking, but also about sharing happiness, joy, and love, and it is also the finest hobby.

C

H

E

F

"GRILLED CHICKEN"

Cookery NC II

Cookery NC II

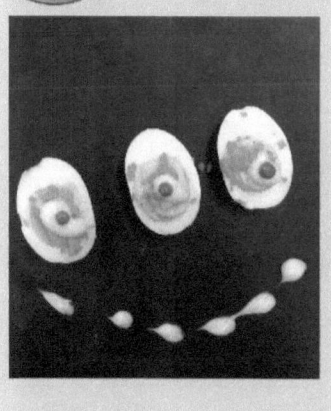

Bread and Pastry Production NC II

"Cooking is something I like doing for a variety of reasons. First and foremost, it is a pleasurable and calming exercise. It makes me delighted to see that the meal I prepared looks and tastes delicious. It's also quite fulfilling to know that I can cook something excellent without the assistance of anyone else. Cooking helps me to express my creativity as well as my culinary talents."

Green peas pasta

Salads

Hazel Bautista Quiamas Simply Recipes Cookbook

For me, the secret of a good cook is not about the butter or herbs and spices you add in a dish. It's about love. Loving what you do, and Making the best that you can.

I love cooking because cooking is like science at the same time an art. Science because when you cook it involves heat, just like chemistry when you Mix different kinds of ingredients, you can create your own recipe. It is an art because when you cut the different kinds of vegetables you can create your own design, you create your own art work. And cooking Is a universal language of love you can express your love and care to those people you love, and it gives you joy and fulfillment when you cook. Creating a dish is like traveling in the past, when you taste the every detail of the food you can remember your loves ones, who first teach you to cook, or the happy moments of your life.

I think cooking is an expression of love,
It is an art, it is a treasure. It's about the culture,
Of the land you came from, it's about family, and
It is in the blood that runs in every vein of your hands.

Hazel B. Quiamas

Bread and Pastry

18 Hazel Bautista Quiamas Simply Recipes Cookbook

Cookery NC II

Cookery NC II

Cookery NC II

Cooking is an essential life skill that everyone should have. It can be a rewarding and enjoyable experience, or it can be a chore. However, learning to cook can be a terrific way to impress your friends and family with your culinary skills. There are numerous cooking ways, so there is bound to be something for everyone. Cooking is a talent that you can always improve on, whether you're a novice or a great chef. Without a question, cooking a meal for someone you care about is a terrific way to express your creativity, and it can be incredibly gratifying. Cooking is a really fulfilling activity. Not only do you get to make something tasty, but you also get to spend time with your friends.

Hazel Bautista Quiamas

Japanese Cuisine

26 Hazel Bautista Quiamas Simply Recipes Cookbook

Japanese

HAZEL BAUTISTA QUIAMAS

For me, the secret of a good cook is not about
the butter or herbs and spices you add in a dish.
It's about love. Loving what you do, and
Making the best that you can.

I love cooking because cooking is like science at the same time an art.
Science because when you cook it involves heat, just like chemistry when you
Mix different kinds of ingredients, you can create your own recipe.
It is an art because when you cut the different kinds of vegetables you can
create your own design, you create your own art work, And cooking Is a
universal language of love you can express your love and care to those people
you love, and it gives you joy and fulfillment when you cook, Creating a dish is
like traveling in the past, when you taste the every detail of the food you can
remember your loves ones, who first teach you to cook, or the happy moments of
your life.

I think cooking is an expression of love,
It is an art, it is a treasure. It's about the culture,
Of the land you came from, it's about family, and
It is in the blood that runs in every vein of your hands.

Hazel B. Quiamas

About the Author

Hazel Bautista Quiamas

Im Hazel Bautista Quiamas I am a trainer in Cookery NC II, Bread and Pastry NC II and Commercial Cooking NC III. Its my fourth book under Ukiyoto Publishing my first Book was Recuerdos de Mi Cerebro, next was the Wisdom Tooth and Accident of my Imagination.

Galley

CIMATECH enterprises turnover power probe diagnostic tool kit to TESDA

Turn over of diagnostic tool kit by CIMATECH to TESDA head of the TESDA Women's Center

The CIMATECH Enterprises, Inc. donated to the TESDA Women's Center power probe electrical diagnostic tools worth PhP82,600.00. The tools were intended to enhance TESDA's capability in training automotive electrical diagnostic for the trainees of the TESDA Women's Center by utilizing the modern equipment. Also, the testing tool kit can be used for the skills training in motorcycle small engine servicing. The kit has the following special features: designed for complete automotive electrical testing; able to work on hybrid vehicle systems safely; able to determine health of motors, relays, lights, wires, sensors, fuel injectors and computer driver; and cuts down the turnaround time in finding electrical faults in any motor vehicle.

The ceremonial turnover of the tools was held on August 29, 2017 at the Tandang Sora Hall, TESDA Women's Center. During the ceremony, the CIMATECH officials announced the conduct of Training of Trainers on the use of the power probe testing kit.

In her welcome message, Ms. Maria Clara B. Ignacio, TWC Chief said that the knowledge on the use of the power probe diagnostic tool kit will increase the employability of the trainees. "Let us be excited to use this tool kit, you are the first to use such tool kit, so if you have competencies on its use, it is a plus factor for you. You maximize your learning by using this tool kit and be motivated to complete your training here at the TESDA Women's Center," said Ms. Ignacio. She expressed optimism for the women automotive trainees "I am sure if you go for work overseas, your knowledge on the use of this electrical diagnostic tool kit will be an added value to your acquired competencies because you will be more empowered."

The CIMATECH Enterprises President, Mr. Edward Jose delivered his message. He expressed thanks and appreciation to the TESDA Women's Center for having been given the opportunity to share this technology from the U.S. through Mr. Melvin del Puerto, representative of the Power Probe. He shared about the product launch: "We launched this in July 2017 at the SMX Center, and we had very good results because companies such as Mitsubishi, Honda, Isuzu, and Nissan want this equipment because it can defect issues in short span of time. The companies were surprised how the tool can work very effectively, very efficiently and very short span of time."

The TESDA MuntiParLas TaPat District Director, Cecilia Amaro, in her message, expressed her aspiration: "I hope you can also share this advertisement about this new technology to other TESDA institutions. We have about 13 institutions offering Automotive Servicing in our district that needs this technology. We can recommend them to adopt this technology, and even to the private industries because we want our trainees to be more employable." She encouraged the trainees to use the tool kit wisely. Finally, she expressed thanks to CIMATECH: "Let us thank these people for sharing to us this technology for us to improve our training delivery."

The occasion was graced by the following officials from CIMATECH, namely: Mr. Edward Jose, President; Mr. Tonyo Calado, General Sales Manager; Mr. Ernest Paguia, Marketing Manager; Ms. Marisse Aromin, Account Executive; and JP Dela Rosa, Technical Sales. From the Power Probe, Mr. Melvin del Puerto, Consultant for SEA, and Mr. Gerald Taban, Sales Trainer, attended the event. District Director Cecilia Amaro and TESDA Women's Center Chief accepted the donated tools by CIMATECH.

Cookery trainee garners 2nd place in free style Korean cooking

She garnered 2nd place in the contest Hazel Quiamas, graduate of Cookery NC II, at the TESDA Women's Center

The contest involved making a single-menu Korean food, participated by Hazel Quiamas, graduate of Cookery NC II, at the TESDA Women's Center. She prepared and cooked Japchae with a twist. "It was a Japchae with a twist of paprika, salted eggs, lemon and chili powder. It was my first time to join a cooking contest," said Hazel.

"Each participant has to prepare two servings of the dish. Cooking and preparation of the dish must be made and done within one hour only. Recipe and taste comprised 70 percent, while presentation made up 30 percent," recalls Hazel.

"I was the first to finish cooking the dish, then the tasting and interview portion followed. I was also inspired with the support of my Trainer Ms. Charmaine Fider and some of my classmates who were there during the contest," said Hazel.

She garnered 2nd place in the contest and received P10,000.00 plus trophy and loot bag with various Korean food products. The contest was organized by the Korean Cultural Center and held at the Lyceum University, Culinary Institute, Intramuros, Manila on July 29, 2017.

Hazel was a Pharmacy student before she enrolled in Cookery NC II at the TWC. Now, she teaches Bread and Pastry, and Food and Beverage Services to Grade 12 students at the Arellano University.

"I have a passion for cooking and I also love to watch cooking shows, cooking movies and documentaries. Also, we have a small eatery business, and I explore food. With cooking, I can express myself by preparing a dish for my family. For me, cooking is like an art. When I cut vegetables, I can create my own art work. By mixing different ingredients, I can create my own recipe," Hazel gladly shared.

30   Hazel Bautista Quiamas Simply Recipes Cookbook

34   Hazel Bautista Quiamas Simply Recipes Cookbook

www.ingramcontent.com/pod-product-compliance
Lightning Source LLC
LaVergne TN
LVHW041559070526
838199LV00046B/2047